THE NEW SUN TIME

ISH KLEIN

CANARIUM BOOKS
NEW YORK CITY, MARFA, ATLANTA

SPONSORED BY
COLUMBIA UNIVERSITY
SCHOOL OF THE ARTS

THE NEW SUN TIME

Canarium Books
New York City, Marfa, Atlanta
www.canarium.org

The editors gratefully acknowledge
Columbia University School of the Arts
for editorial assistance and generous support.

Cover: Photograph of the solar eclipse of
May 29, 1919, by Arthur Stanley Eddington.

First Edition

Printed in the United States of America

ISBN 13: 978-1-7344816-0-0

CONTENTS

To Life

SATANIC RITES OF THE, UH, DRACULA

These rites are on computer everywhere.
    Cool people are in furry vests, the past.
Someone's delirious; he got the rope
off. Vest didn't notice and then: crazy.
If he's frozen, he is sitting one out.

He's getting out of the house, control room's
notified. They're rubbing the red crosses
off. Gin. Skin—red leather, yellow leather.
"You're sure it was Cole Porter?" The cockerel?
There's an IV drip in the reel to reel

room. Oh! He's a spy. Photos in his watch.
… put your foot wrong and you'll probably join …
An officer under ground cover. Was
Joan Crawford really there? Precincts of Hades.
Imperial general staff: ladies

naked ladies. The six thousand terrors
of hell, by them. Collecticking spiders.
He could dissolve this office with a nod
of his head. This department, that's what I
said. D.D. Denham, he's money. He's it.

Behind the chemicals, oil and bank.
Long shot—tree in field, background cows. Two suave
men, one suave woman in a fur coat. Smoke.
Questioning the colonel we find he's dead.
The twenty-third of this month—a guy dies

macho—his eyes open. Peter Cushing
adding a cross to silver, looking through
binoculars. A silver cross melted
into a bullet. Dreamy music. "It's
a sniper get down!" Why did he have that

wood-cut image of the Dracula, ah,
on his wall? How did Peter get—"Jessie
he's only playing with us he could pick
us out at any time." They'll save Jessie.
They knock out NoName. Earmarked for later

Sailor at the desk has geraniums.
Security. "You are to go up to
his private apartment. No cameras."
Denham is, uh, Dracula, probably.
Cut to the injured parties on the floor.

No camera, just a little pistol.
Away from Denham. "I've been expecting
you ever since Julian Keely took his
own life." "The decadence of the present
day can and will be halted." The unhole—

pardon, unholy, aura about this
place a.k.a. Vempiricism, bad
habits help you concentrate—tobacco.
Peter drops a bible, slyly. Am I
to suffer the same fate as Professor

Keely? Christopher Lee, I mean, D.D.
     Meanwhile, everything was done exactly
as you commanded; in return you must—
(He broke a beaker of plague in his hand).
Industrialist catches the plague fast.

The colonel is dead. I know, I said that.
A bad hippy is electrocuted.
They upend a table. "My revenge is
spread over centuries and it's just begun."
Four industrialists burn. Hawthorne branch

for protection, Lorimer Van Helsing
and Peter Cushing run into the bush.
"He wants to pollute this world and spread death
and decay so that he can finally
die." Well, that's one way. Later he takes up

Chris' ring. Now, it's all about desire.
He calls out "Dracula—" stabbing. He's like
at last, at last, at last, at last, at last.
Blossom fallen from a branch returned as
butterfly does that make sense?

Everything tangled—the edges of images—

It's like they play hide and seek with us,

old lands do on their way to the new.

TRIALS

Friends, in 1386 a sow is executed in the public square
dressed like a man. It is written. People swear.

In 1587 a case was filed against beetles
ravaging vineyards. Bring them in to hear the document.
It says, leave our district—we give you three days.

Last trial in France 1741 a cow executed.
I think she licked the man's crotch in a harrowing way—
they say this ruined the milk and poisoned the children.

In England a dog was tried near Chichester, 1771.
Who won? I do not know now—

All-communicating old world can you see me?

In 1891 Leland said, they tried to exorcize
the Colorado beetle in America.
Call the wren the king of birds
for they will eat the beetles.

I say unto you. Grow up for this—
to call the—well why do you laugh?

Are you a Leyden jar?
Are you just? The Leyden jar—

capacitors and visuals.
Bees, bees awake.
Protective shape—the crescent moon.

The wave of the shape, the wave of the sound—
What? Who shot a wild black rabbit? That was our grandma.

He shot who—she shot her grandma—she shot our grandma.
What? Who shot her? they did, wait who? what?

Into the grass—is this a wolf, a hawk, a cat, a fox, a dog?

Can you find someone who can still see you without your gun?

May we please see the skull, exhibit A?

How long has he had this thing?

How much flesh does one get to keep?

How much did you have at first?

Working? Is that advanced flesh?

Do you know what is an ovary?

Some holding close, others letting

the fruit fall. When there is some fruit left

like for who—and how much? and what?

the ground—the air you breathe not a hand bag or epoxy

I don't have to go to hell with you, man, but I can tell

you've got it in you. The change that deranges us.

I have flipped

The G will change to C. Please note—it can be

if you had a chance—if there is somewhat a chance to care

beyond you that's your chance

now that you are gone but for want—

who do you care for when you think about it, chrysanthemum?

Please tell the court and be clear.

THE DEPTH OF THE COAL

The Depth of the coal
by which I mean, the depth of the cool.
The Depth was knowing at the string of me
by which I mean last Thursday.

Is a peaceful life what I am doing here?
Women are talking about you
which means you will not die today.
A face with a name is made

from every single person who looked through
the eyes assigned to your name there.
Glaucous, Blurry, By Sugar Harmed,
Blue from a flipped perception of water,

Brown from going for the gold. If the pressing
of the lenses throws the book at you,
or says the words <<sacré pieds>>,
let's just say yellow over blue, Fool.

I feel a funeral is implied. I gripe inside
when people cry. Why not bounce a ball?
My concern that they are snagging
the progress of the choice with pointed misery.

What's confusing is not that nobody owns anything really

but that the all is free.
A custom I began in my mind is to put the corpse
on a blanket the loved ones each taking an edge
and bouncing the corpse as if to say if this ain't fun,

get with loving faces.

Bet. The first guy splattered with embalming
fluid will say "fuck this I'm done." Or maybe
that was me. Let me stop. The best I can do
is to not be cool to you by which I mean

indifferent. And I'm vexed at the disregard
for animal skin. There are others like me.
In french the word is embêté.
"Holmes, do you think there is a link?

Insofar as this here word rhymes with empathy?"
"Watson are you making fun of me?"
"No Holmes, just the one thing; not *of* you."
"Watson you are a fool. Now give me the key to my room."

"Guess which hand."
"With you
it's always the left."
"Correct."

Perhaps you have experienced
jealousy at the funeral
for the man who is dead.
I felt it myself.

I responded to the stabbing; the woman
found me and gave me meat and material.
She said I should find my family
(wasn't that you?)

I finish our interaction eleven years later.
Oh good one. Oh good, that's done.
"Holmes, what do you make of the concept
of the double one; or ten and one,
the word we call eleven?

Could this be the real meaning
of the complete face and the very, very
different face beside it?
We see it beside ourselves.

Holmes!

Holmes!

I know you're in there

I can smell your pipe smoke!"

BUILDINGS OF TOMORROW TODAY

We're not a house anymore. We're
an apartment in a building.
This apartment is collapsing.

Top floor? Course not. More collapsing.
That we are in the vast middle;
like the cashier said, "nobody."

I forget if I'm right or left
handed. I must be near the top.
Someone is collapsing on me.

In the seventies, mobile homes
were stacked vertically. The frame
was from the so-called third world steel.

Over-frame holding each unit.
The stairs often gave out and cheap
PVC pipes were supposed to

save us from lead poisoning. Space
but no silence. The floor over
that guy, his anxiety-in-

duced accent. Chemical treatment.
A sort of steel frame for one's own
brain. I'm negative. Cytomeg-

alovirus negative. I
have given much of my blood to
babies and folks with no immune

system. I know that I'm bragging.
It's because I can't anymore.
Why are the vikings still alive?

There is now fake blood; I've tried it.
There's a steroid chaser so it's
tricky. Can you change your serum

by yourself in a permanent
way. Genuine? It's not red like
the old stuff, many hands made it

to live with, or in or over.

INSURANCE

Was I a jerk at the hospital? Was I whining?
If I were Doctor Hardass would I, to me, be
like: you deserve a gulag. You know no real pain.
You got mom problems. Wrong. I'm mad at liars and finks.

I'm nice. Being honest is nice. Fuck you.
In the hospital booth, they won't cover us.
It costs a lot. Is it worth it? Consider the unborn.
They say, their base is in Kentucky. What's Kentucky

got to do with over here? Take a look at the area:
dead lottery tickets, a big healthy rat by a tire rim,
purple crocuses planted 13 years ago. They're the heroes.
A store gives away samples of birthday cake,

yellow cake with blue icing among the fudge.
Bumper stickers like: Human be Good! & Laugh!
Does this help my wish to get us a sandwich
on a regular or predictable basis?

Someone lied about sandwiches saying they were veggie.
Mine had lamb even though I told them I'm a vegetarian.
I couldn't believe it was meat at first. I know you didn't
ask, but I thought I'd tell you what it's like for us here.

GEOMAGNETIC REVERSALS

At the laundromat the earth shifted its
polarity. A child went missing. "… always
lots of fights at the gas station." (Gas = Fighting?)
Knife throwing and drug use reported.

Today in response to missing children
and the missing children epidemic
I hear, "Search yourself. Search your own damn self."
While you wait, replacement windows installed.

This morning's report: daffodils: oh yes!
They are very successful separatists.
And then when I trace their path to this dirt
now, it has to be admitted: they know.

The human extinction is parts of mind's
contacts lost. A piece of a hyacinth
alive but of a diminished form. It
came up like that. On the west side, one more

crash; it's a school bus. (I will check the grass.)
From this, laws for drivers will toughen up.
And by the dirt in the crash sight grows mint:
increasing every year; some new today.

LOST PEOPLE HERE AND FURTHER ON
OUT IN THE FOG

When X said that one was naked, one was talking
out loud alone. One lost her, uh, inhibition
or didn't frame—they're talking to sing, for instance.

Over there they sing at night within parameters.
Get it all out, the rationale. Talking to air
in our group zone. The part of the house we call blue

room or wet. What do other people do? How much do you
have to eat? Is everyone talking
to computers. Malcolm X said in his youth

they called a job a "slave." They're right.

I'm calling the clouds to come down so no
one can take aim at you, X. And I hate when they
laugh mean like ha ha ha ha, ho ho ho ho, hee hee

hee hee, huh huh huh, huh. Feel better? No. Gimme
a can opener. I need the feeling of opening.
Buster was a can opener too. He does it with moves,

the mad cap moves. I've got an army version on my key ring.
A P-38. Take cue from the instant
hole. Open up. That's right. Under hand. Nice and slow.

See that opening? Rise and
go through.

HOW TO RUN A-
MOK WITH PICTURES

In the cornfield
amid the rows

I grind my teeth.
In the empty
concert hall I
fail. It was not

empty. I do
not run. True em-
pty places cause
heavy signals

from our bodies.
Love this or find
them. They are in
the coffee bars

and reading rooms.
In libraries
they are at the
edge of the street.

They, them, you are
crowds in theory.
When I do not
stop talking I

run amok. Why
not be quiet?
An assertion
of my life, may-

be. I talk on
Greenview near Far-
go. See me o-
pen my mouth? This

photo with a
cloud that is on
my face proves the
fifth dimension.

To get a pict-
ure, have a strong
thought visually
expressed. God, I

love talking to
no one really.
I feel so loved.
Like when my ex-

friend called me ev-
eryday five
times at least. We
joked about how our

fantasies were
mating with deer,
for example.
Or themselves deer.

What a relief
someone knew a-
bout the ani-
mals in danger.

INVISIBLE WINDOWS

Oh, the website of cheap torso.   I'll meet you
there. Image of a square next to a larger square
in each of which are   a rectangle, a stick figure,

incorporating,   mentally,   another   stick,   scribble
scrabble and the z's. When the stick figures leave
they   go   "Adios   Bitcheros!"   Witty   but   will

their body get some spheres and arches? I will worry
about that for 10 more seconds.   Growing pains are
upon the point of me   and my line. I am stiff.

What ever happened to my electric company exposé?
Here it is: the company steals money from customers
through opaque transmissions fees.   Same with the

telecommunications   and   they're all   in   bed
with Collections Agencies.   Who are our government.
I put my funds into "Peoples United."   Why not?

I'm one of us; an essentialized   surface going out.
I can believe it. I could believe it. And I will
have that as a stick of gum. Fractal? How one is

stuck with what one learned right out the front door.
The two prime movers and their zone.   Your
walls.   That is a hard limit.   Unless they were

everyone. Like the pictures.   Could that be okay?
To lose one's fear of being burned by a mob, you
have to be of a mob that wouldn't burn others. Cinema

Village. Certain pictures prove my point; others have
what is known as subtext. Personal Shadow when I met
you at the website, you did not look like you look now:

for one thing, you had no head, just a torso costumed
with a hangover shirt. I figured we'd meet up again.
In which website was your head?   Is it not being

considered properly citizen?   Is this why it is out
of the interaction area?   I'm sorry if your personal
citizenship idea has been destabilized for years.

On the movie screen are computerized faces. They used
to be simple people. When dead, a guy's story goes on.
It is content.   While alive we could have known them.

I try to like, as much as possible;   the ones I can
be with. What is the   alternative? Spend my life
making a chair valuable for the view it provides into

the lives of the ones on the screen who are already
gone   gone
gone

JACK BENNY, SPECTER, THE DISK OF PLEASURE

In "The Treasury of Modern Humorists," George Burns said that
he was the best comedian because he could break Jack Benny up.
What?! Jack Benny, the man the boy in me
was built for. You are wrong

George. I have always found you unfunny to a fault.
Your wife, a cute puppy which I mean with malice. George Burns,
how could you who are limited in every apparent way move Jack?
Jack the bear to my soft Goldilocks.

Let us stroll among the windmills out here (my mind).
I'll get my little light. See, we have many specters.
Quiet, I multiply. In this fantasy mist I am a beautiful lad
on the balcony of an L.A. love pad. Jack's hotel!

I'm stuck, what's holding us up? Shit, it's Mary, the Front.
Now see Jack as appeasement monkey. Thee Jack Benny!
See the watery baby blues inside the meaty head. What's this?
Him saying, "Now don't be silly, of course there's no one else."

I'm in underpants. It's chilly. Inside I see his shoulders going
up like that upstart Ed Sullivan. He sees me.
"Get down, get down." the hand sign and Mary exits. That was
Mary Livingston, ladies and gentlemen, off to make Jell-O.

Opens the sliding door. Oh yes. I go, "Hi."

"Now you... I don't want any trouble." He says while backing up.

Sure he does. I am hustled upstairs.

Roughly, thank God.

Back before I had this hotel I was bugged by many Bennyesque men

and I maintain a soft spot.

It squeaks, "Love me, love me, love me,

you seem susceptible and mean." I like that they can't help it.

Thing about Jack is he's a nice guy and wants to help me.

"Why don't you go back to school?" He often asks.

"Well..."

Weird how this affects my respect in a lowering way.

Like his wish for words of love.

"Goldie," he pinches my lips open from below,

"say you love your big bad bear."

"Now Jackson, you know I need the threatening incentive."

Suddenly the cock is sideways feeling, retracting.

"You mean you don't really love me? Even though I've projected

myself from death to the wind-milled fields above Philadelphia?"

"Back up, Jackson. What was the question?"

"Well if you're not even following—
Oh what's the use?" Off he storms. A radio sound effect. Shoes
to the door that slams! That was Jack Benny, ladies and gentle-
men, breaking for Jell-O and maybe a Lucky Strike.

Well...
The ever-present disk of pleasure shifts further away.
Some nights I jump off this balcony to catch the edge of it.
I hang on until nausea forces me to release. Flung then am I

into the Los Angeles air. It is before the war in a neighborhood
where no one gets lynched or unwillingly humiliated.
I levitate and kick back down.
Way down to shuffling street level.

Enter dimension two
where the Gracie Allens sweetly scoot around.
They are little puppies or disgusting toddlers.
Damn them! If one comes up, I will stomp it down

then watch it incompletely re-inflate.
It will limp after me, but I will leave it!
That's me giving experience. So?
Have you never?

Relax, I am not now stomping.
I'm detached actually.
The Great Oz, not at all.
I jump to get cut by the edge

of the pleasure disk: Round Saw! And up
and up for more cuts. And the men and the squeaky females
and the lovable cuddly things… oh so what?
I'm not even here. I'm not even hearing them. Well.

MORPHOLOGY OF THE COUCH AND MISTRESS

In the life before this life. I suppose—
well, that's one way to drive oneself nuts.
The life before this life really can't count.
Even if you feel surrounded by them.
Our couch cannot feel pleasure. The mistress.

Listen: that wasn't it. Listen: now. Wait.
Listen, the servant girl is the mistress in
reverse. The mistress is servant too, or
listen, this mistress-servant thing depends
on those who would be mistress or servant.

Listen/vocal throat, a freedom outside.
Listen, I must not say "you" because "you"
are someone of an unknown quantity
kind of like the "I." And too quality.
Not mine to manage, not mine to define.

Our couch cannot feel pleasure because-ful.
The first part of that "ful" reads unsuccess.
The couch expected. Isn't that right, couch?
"I met someone from France, it messed with me."
"Why France? Are they the elves?" "They are not elves."

"You are gonna have to do better than that, (couch)."
"Well then it was a romantic movie."
"Nobody ever stays here anyway." Good God,
the couch is always on. And hot!
Commenting on people who do things on or near itself,

uh, herself. Partner bought her from an Art
dealer. I met her before she budded.
I never owned my own couch. I got a room.
Listen, I like the way there is no dog
smell around, no saliva leaking out.

I like that language sound. Not my language.
I do think "servant" is a faulty con-
cept. Are the hands just spoons? The mouth a drain?
I would say not normally. I would be
still. Or practice laziness for freedom.

To confirm it while having "nothing." Though "nothing?"
Be serious. Am I right?
Listen, One has muscle plus secretions and
sequestering what runs off this massive
hand. The mind of the hole works with that task.

A lot of sun today. I want some so-
lar. Will I be dragged downstairs and out
the front door for this desire and if
so, subject myself to the ones who take
the fabric and the batting and the wood?

Non-visual bubbling is grandchildren.
Glad hopping becomes rapid shifts to grief.
Couch tendency being continual
and too an avid woman overhead.
She gave me a blue book with gold pages.

By which I mean, thanks.

THE PREMISE OF HANDS

"Ignorance," said the program
"(because I do not want to listen to you)."
Oh sphere of influence and I, a class under, his hand
trying to pull out every last strand of my hair.

You have to think fast when this happens.
I said, "To every strand a hand!" and then
"Go high, go low but don't go with him!"
I foresaw his kibble dinner.

A fetish from what his sister fed her dolls.
They were pretty—little cylinders in a pile. The Alps.
But then I was with him.
One hand/one strand the indestructible one under his collar.

Assessments persistently rude
come from strict programming.
Sometimes in isolation
they say to run

for example, what I thought were life-sized
toys (mirrors of force),
were isolations begetting isolations.
Capable of violin?

On my way to sleep an important pixel
for the picture wants to cry.
A face making an ugly example of crying.
I can't not No.

I. Not no I not. Why not?
Laugh, that'll get him.
Unclosing I. You are sucking up
for what? Dresses are out of control.

A soul that is made by endeavor.
The premise of two particular hands
having hands. Am I a reliable source?

I will not say, "I will see you tomorrow."
Another pixel in the picture cuts out.
"Not a pixel but an image off a side of sand."

I said.

And he was like, where?
and I was like light
and he was like contagious stupidity

and I was like nice

and he was like when are you leaving?

and I was like when I'm ready

and he was like offended

and I was like you want me to do the German version

   of lick your asshole though you insult me

and he was like you are a prostitute in German

and I was like your mother is a prostitute

and he said destroy me in German

and I said I'd like to see him try

and he was like, breaking up,

   the crummy room

and I was like crying

and he was like "nice"

and I said the only thing I like

   about you is your ladies underpants.

   Everything else is shit.

Infections of people—

Do I miss me without you?

But I know where that guy is.

A person has to move

above or beneath the face of what they do
and what they say they do
and what the others say they do and what is done

for a change
as if a change.

Iamb, iamb, iamb, iamb, iamb alive

hearts are, I want to say a nice flip side.

That dead guy—why can't
I let him go?
All he does is hate us.
A problem I must notice:

how intensely a dog cares.

COMPENSATION FROM THE RINGS OF SATURN

Here comes my cube. And now the box
in which a room. 'Round town they play

in the pool. Am I jealous of
playing? Sort of. I laugh in the

house sometimes. Before a baby.
Babies are fine. They can't help it.

The last great joke. Moses asking
Jesus if he wanted to play golf

or just fuck around. Ask me for
details later. Okay—a hawk

a little bunny rabbit, a
hole. Who did you say took you? The

hawk, yes he has decayed teeth. Could
he help it? He was playing holes

with rabbits and squirrels. Like minions.
Saturn: the distance I was from

the game, the Jesus, in the joke.

U

In this one: the botchelliskic cans and glowing
dials. What were they doing with so much arsenic?

And why are all these good bicycles here? Did they
have no room? A homeopath on sepia

fights the falling uteruses. Says, "I'll get them
back." Most of the uterus is sick of him. They

know. A precious necklace rings heart and breast. A peach
can and its label on the beach. Made it! Some act

in migrations among matter. We see a show
where nice people are pushed too far. Pushed too far? On

a moving train? A faith based in uranium.
At the dinner party, one gets a lighting by

the big necklace. It's better to be in the light.
The necklace says the dump has particles who can

penetrate any place. By place the necklace means
people. The necklace seems happy about that. Word

has it a heart hangs under its perimeter.

A lot of what she says feels like a test.

Like, for instance: which part of U is beauty for me?

DAISY'S DAISIES

A friendliness: circle, dot, dot, curve
or a dove, a cactus and a cookie.
Is to hold to kill?

High protein hash of dove with cactus.
Who will eat that?
Are they sucking butter to be young?

Does the end of butter give rise to trees?
Do I love the bear's frown
like possible future?

Shut up is a loved one: a half-brown evergreen.
And vocal suspicions: a shaking,
a stepping on the ground which is suspicious.

In that book, to evergreen: to say the same thing again
and again and again and again, is not a problem.
Remember oneself remembering; instances opening.

The figures called emojis.
A phone, one up-pointing thumb, a fingernail being painted,
filled in it is a silhouette of a coughing head.
What do you make of a tiny figure in a red dress

bending her elbows and sticking out her foot?
Talk about your mealy pears.
Talk about your medlars and abnormally soft types.

Look who turns up next to the road where a great daisy
had been. These are clouds and also wings
where have they been?

TODAY A SEDGE WREN

The Mess, the Sedge Wren—
Play, mash primer, hide

a dial. A man with
men and swords: dials.

No cycle goes smooth.
Today a mess: bird

in the backyard men
a fire to send

every element
from integrity.

No subject rather
it is a vortex.

Them. They're not you. Build
and snoop. High fire.

Not a man you know.

Hide.

WHAT CAN HAPPEN NEXT?
KNIFE VS. NOSE

I live in a room.
How this happened? Look,
I know I'm lucky. Nose.
Arnold Horseshack says
his show was cancelled.

"It's devastating
they loved me and now——?"
I let myself go
and now what, now what?
Juan Epstein and I

have gone our own ways.
Separately? Yes, yes.
I loved to hate him.
Him, being a knife——
Is there a fan club?

What can happen next?
Ben Gazzara says
he is not a knife.
He's Italian,
come on, don't be dumb.

Ric Ocasek says
he is not the knife.
He has his own shit
that he must deal with.
I remember when

hair loss was my fear.
Certain nurses say
bathe your head with grease.
Just do it knife-boy
and read Foucault, bitch.

Angel came apart.
Models get hooked: yes.
Sometimes turn starlet.
That is what "let" means.
Led to this puppet

and how you don't know:
as above so long
suckers below or
middle finger and
then what? Hawaii?

Noses don't touch those
rocks. Crowds on your side?
What? "You are a pig"
he said in answer
to her refusing

him. He's his knife crotch.
Starlets your noses
can be your best friends.
They are for you too.
Have nose for your self.

It's out there somewhere.
Reason demands it.
I speak to my star.
Eve is like Rhoda
confident and kind.

Nolte's in the park.
They say he's clean now.
I would say hello.
What else? I don't know.
We could eat a samosa.

Felix's brother
met John and Yoko
on the astral plane.
He said they were nice.
Really, really nice.

This tells me something.
Eh, allowing love
for it is outside
very like the nose.
A lovely huge nose.

I met Moishe K.
he was love and nose.
He could teach Nolte.
He's busy. I think.
I fear they're busy.

I saw D. Hannah
in the park after
I had broke my nose.
She had sympathy.
She's real lovable.

We are far away.
This room is outside.
Kind of like a pen.
I do walk out though.
D. Bowie came to

a thing I was in.
He laughed like a kid.
I'm lucky for that.
I'll come to your show.
I will love your nose.

BUILT ALONG THE LINES OF A FINE NIGHT

Roses? No. Parameters. A person newly
situated. "You're a chump if you get—"

That area points into me "taken in."

AKA "Don't leave me." Or: "Ooh, ho,
ho so you're a sucker fish?" I can hear it.

Shut up. I tell me not you. I am taking
this to go from point A to point b.

Dust extracted from a comb by a card that says
"depot." These recordings are how I was seeing.

Dear Chief Inspector, something about us
wants to be literate in the dark dark.

To be free people freeing the people stuck
to us. Getting the crude oil off our skins.

Everybody knows skin's important.

They're coming over, time to hide.
Maybe I'm not the best deputy.

Later, I'll run in the middle of the night
to prove I'm not afraid of running

in front of someone who would
look out their window late at night.

Can I play a game while sleeping? Can I love?
I like smurfs because they come from mushrooms.

The world is full of miracles; toys
are our blueprints for better living.

To make a beautifully moving smurf or a soft
system of Legos a guy could actually eat.

"If you meet the right people, you can make it!"

And get free giving it all to the world!
Wait! No. Yes! I have a need for this, I think.

I can be a meeting; make a meeting here.
It seems to be raining. I'll shovel the ice.

Greg comes through here and I don't want him to slip.
If I bring in sticks, tonight a fire.

Two nights ago it would have been too late.

EVERY ANIMAL IS YOUR MOTHER

There's a park in the West where

Grizzly Bear is eaten
by no one. They will eat
rodents, insects, elk, calves,
carrion, pine nuts, large
mammals, berries, roots and
grasses. They are ready.

rivers wish to take the rings.

Black Bears eat rodents,
insects, elk, calves, pine nuts,
grasses, carrion, berries
and a plant we've not met.
Black bears may live inside
wolves, grizzly bears, mountain

Not happy. Not not happy.

lions and humans as
food. To be eaten by
a Grizzly Bear if you
are a black bear, well, I

just think that'd be weird: Bears!
Doing it their own way.

And outside the wild range.

Elk eat grasses, sedges,
apsen bark, acquatic
plants and shrubs. They must run
from wolves, grizzly bear, mountain
lions and humans. How they keep
going is a wonder.

Those caught wish to return home.

The Red Foxes eat beetles
grasshoppers, grains, berries
crickets, nuts, mice—not all
at once—they hide some for
later like you and me.
They are prey to bobcats,

To be alive for instance.

lynx, mountain lions and
wolves. The Red Fox tells

their pups they are the best
foxes when they feed them
rabbits, birds, turtles, eggs,
and even the road kills.

Life rises around bars briefly.

The Beaver eats grasses,
sedges, inner tree bark—
that's the list! Meanwhile,
wolves, bears, scavengers
and humans will eat them!
They deserve a refund.

It's all bars until you can leave.

Bighorn Sheep eat grasses
and shrubby plants perhaps
they do not sweat the wolves,
coyote, and humans
who will eat them. The Sheep
see it as their next phase.

I remember what I love.

Mountain Lion eat elk,
mule deer, and small mammals.
Nothing listed eats them.
They are in ultimate phase
before becoming or
eating a human spore.

Independent, independent

We don't exactly know how
the brain works. The Snow
Shoe Hare eats conifer
needles and shrubs. They're prey
to lynx, foxes, bobcats,
great horned owls, coyote—

situation, situation.

Enfolded in this way,
some may think the Snow Shoe
Hare is effed. On the run
all the time. Their debts or
obligations rising
over them on the grass.

Is freedom a loving state?

I do not! Buds and twigs
are eaten by Snow Shoe
Hares and by moose, deer, elk
and beavers. Buds and twigs
seem to be trying to
help or end in a bear.

Is loving a freedom state?

We wish to go to Space!
Not everyone. Cultured
fruits are et in space. Bears,
birds, foxes, deer, insects,
and coyotes will put
wild fruit in their guts.

All material has will.

Aspen is food to elk,
beaver, insect and that's
all. Paper is their night-
mare. Veneer of mixed years
subject to a meaning.

Post life experience.

Shifts within and out: lightning.

Grasses who rule the dirt
are eaten by elk, deer,
bears, moose, rodents and insects.
Young Grass on the mountain
wasting them poisons air
and water for humans.

From Light my mind starts again.

Snakes eat small rodents, fish,
salamander, frogs, worms,
insects and tadpoles. They
are et by fish, birds, and
carnivorous mammals
while being undidactic.

From Light I remain myself.

Birds are eaters of seeds,
insects, berries and fish.
They'll be et by other

birds and carnivorous
mammals and snakes. The squirrels
and weasels eat their eggs.

Flooding Light: flooding edge light—

Aquatic Insects eat
aquatic insects—others –
and detritus. They are
food to amphibians,
fish and birds. What they feel
is known only to them?

The small coils in square mines.

The Eagle eats fish, ducks,
and carrion. Eating
the dead has made them a
majestic question, right?
They live in my state too.
Outrageous to song birds.

Rising, rising, rising.

The Ground Squirrel loves to eat

fungi, roots, leaves, birds' eggs,
buds, insects, carrion,
seeds and nuts. The foxes,
owls, badgers, weasels, hawks
and coyotes eat them.

Completion for every being.

Do you love a Ground Squirrel?
I do not. Do you love
a Flying Squirrel? I do.
I am a nut. The love
is associative. Aspens
are right but I must live!

I must only move towards life.

Deer eat shrubs, conifers,
aspen and grasses. If
they will be eaten, it
will be by humans, bears,
wolves, coyotes, mountain
lions. That's what they want.

Sometimes it is stupid: life!

Terrestrial Insects
eat plant material
other insects and blood.
Rodents, weasels, foxes,
martens, coyotes, fish,
bears and birds eat them—good.

The strings are tiny engines.

The Pika eat grasses,
conifers, sedges, twigs
and lichen. Who will eat
them? Coyote, hawks, pine
martens. Do they know the
Pika eats its own spore?

Trust. Trust? Trust! Trust—Trust...

It's important for health.
We must learn how the brain
works. Manage emotions.
The Glaciers are out there.
How near are we to them?
Our brains are in this earth.

Ancient ghosts are no one's friend.

Weasels eat rodents, snakes,

ground squirrels, insects, birds, frogs,

eggs and they can have fun.

Even though coyote,

hawks, owls, and fox eat them.

Humans are excluded

Who is holding who here?

for what they have done they

have no fun. To trap a

being and take his or

her fur. You have no fun

if you are to do that.

Good luck having no fun.

Do you prefer to eat ants?

River Otters—a crown

of recreation—they

eat fish, frogs, young muskrat.

They are trapped by humans

for fur. The humans pay
and are not allowed to play.

To share is to be respectful.

Learn the world. The words
are not straight. Pine Marten!
lately eating eggs, birds,
rodents, hares, insects, shrews,
berries. Owls may eat them
and humans trap for fur—

I specifically say fur—

Shrews and Moles mainly eat
insects. They are food to
foxes, owls, coyotes
and hawks. Who will digest
the Shrew's hands and nose? Who?
Recordings in the mouth?

Your shape is Bear Shape—upright

Mice eat seeds. That's all they
listed. Mice are very

intelligent which makes
them taste good to owls, hawks,
foxes and coyotes.
They are a supplement.

sometimes but mostly all fours.

Yellow-bellied Marmot
are just omnivorous.
They live in colonies.
Coyote, fox and bears
get their greens by eating
Marmot stomachs and tubes.

Shoulders roll, feet point in.

Coyote eat ground squirrels
with pride and carrion,
small mammals, birds and deer.
Only wolves seem to want
to eat them. Perhaps it's
like silencing a card

There is nothing up my sleeves.

or clown. It does not seem
like a weak move if you
eat them. But when they live
inside—impossible
the grin is bigger than
the mouth like they planned it.

    I am coming from the brain.

Cutthroat Trout eats small fish,
fish, eggs, algae, insects,
frogs and small rodents which
got delivered, I guess.
They're et by bald eagles,
lake trout, otters, osprey—

    I will go towards commotion

and humans. The Wolf eats
hoofed animals mainly,
in fact, 90%.
Nobody eats them for
real. Agents of the grass
rely on their contents.

—I arrive and I want to

Mute Swans eat snails, grasses
aquatic plants, waste grain,
insects and small water
animals. Their young are
preyed upon by raccoons,
mink, foxes, the wolves—

and something beyond the feed corn

planted there. Comes up and comes

around: grass and seed in the earth

are forces born to birth you

as you are born a force of birth.

NOTES

Page 3: *The Satanic Rites of Dracula* is a 1973 Hammer horror film.

Pages 7-10: Some info in this poem, "Trials," was from *Discovering the Folklore of Birds and Beasts* by Venetia Newall.

Page 14: Holmes refers to detective Sherlock Holmes created by Arthur Conan Doyle.

Page 22: This information is in *The Autobiography of Malcolm X*, written by Malcolm X and Alex Haley, 1992 edition.

Page 23: A "P-38" is a tiny can opener developed by the military for rations.

Page 30: Jack Benny was a comedian (1894-1974). I know nothing about his sexuality.

Page 30: George Burns and Gracie Allen were a comedy duo who were also married.

Page 30: Mary Livingstone was Jack Benny's wife.

Page 33: The Great Oz is a character from the movie based on a book by L. Frank Baum.

Page 43: Oblique reference to Ludwig Wittgenstein.

Page 46: *U* is the symbol for Uranium.

Page 49: "Abnormally soft types" is a Charles Fourier classification.

Pages 54-58: Who's Who:

Arnold Horseshack? A character from TV's *Welcome Back Kotter*.

Who is Juan Epstein? A character from TV's *Welcome Back Kotter*.

Who is Ben Gazzarra? An actor (1930-2012).

Who was Ric Ocasek? A musician (1944-2019).

Who is Foucault? A French Philosopher; first name Michel (1926-1984).

What is a Starlet? A situation conforming to contemporary beauty ideals.

Who is Eve? A great playwright, generally.

What is Rhoda? A television show about a woman from the seventies.

What is Nolte? An actor in recovery.

Who is Felix's brother? A visionary.

Who are John and Yoko? They are musicians and Yoko is also an artist.

Who is Moishe K.? A theater luminary.

Who is D. Hannah? An actress and activist.

Who is D. Bowie? A musician and a helpful friend.

Page 60: Smurfs are small blue creatures; they were popular toys in the eighties.

Page 60: Legos are interlocking plastic building blocks.

ACKNOWLEDGMENTS

"The Depth of the Coal" was first published in *Cosmonaut Avenue*.

"Jack Benny, Spectre, the Disk of Pleasure" was first published by *Bridge Magazine* (c.2005).

"Every Animal Is Your Mother" was first published at the online journal *Incessant Pipe*, and then as a chapbook by Factory Hollow Press.

"The Premise of Hands" was published in the *Anthology* of the Departure Readings Series.

"Built Along the Lines of a Fine Night" and "What Can Happen Next?" were first published in *Oversound*.

Thank you friends: Max Winter, John Beer, Clay Ventre, Jon Ruseski, Peter Gizzi, Dara Wier, Nellie Prior, Samuel Amadon, Liz Countrymen, Andy McAlpine, Sarah Beth McAlpine, Jed Berry, Emily Houk, John Sieraki, Mike Wall, Liz Bryne, Arda Collins, Stella Corso, Bryan Beck, Corwin Ericson, David Feinstein, Kendra Weisbin, Jo Grose, Mickle Maher, Pearl Ramsey, Theater Y, Mary Hickman, Robert Fernandez, Val and Jim and Heather and Lily and Delia Pless, Wilson Yerxa, and the brand new people: Isadore, Franklin, and their seniors, Issa, Sacha, Robinson, and Gordon. Thanks Josh, Lynn, Robyn, and Nick for making the book happen and for being so awesome. And thanks Greg you are pretty much always the good life.

Ish Klein is the author of *The New Sun Time*, *Consolation and Mirth*, *Moving Day*, and *Union!*, all published by Canarium Books, and her poems have also appeared in *Triple Canopy*, *Fence*, *jubilat*, *Versal*, on the Poetry Foundation website, and elsewhere. Ish is a founding member of the Connecticut River Valley Poets Theater or CRVPT. Her play, *In A Word, Faust*, has been performed internationally and was published by the *Cambridge Literary Review*. She's also the author of several other plays, including *The Dee Men*, *Drummer 41*, and *The Orchids*, which was a finalist for the Leslie Scalapino Award for Innovative Women Performance Writers.